What's a [illegible] of foreplay?
(see page 2)

What do men and beer bottles have in common?
(see page 32)

What does the perfect male look like?
(see page 49)

What's a man's definition of eternity?
(see page 68)

Why is sleeping with a man like a soap opera?
(see page 96)

Also by Blanche Knott
Published by St. Martin's Press

TRULY TASTELESS JOKES IV
TRULY TASTELESS JOKES V
TRULY TASTELESS JOKES VI
TRULY TASTELESS JOKES VII
TRULY TASTELESS JOKES VIII
TRULY TASTELESS JOKES IX
TRULY TASTELESS JOKES X
TRULY TASTELESS JOKES XI
TRULY TASTELESS JOKES XII
TRULY TASTELESS JOKES XIII
TRULY TASTELESS JOKES XIV
TRULY TASTELESS ANATOMY JOKES
TRULY TASTELESS ANATOMY JOKES II
TRULY TASTELESS DOCTOR JOKES
TRULY TASTELESS LAWYER JOKES
TRULY TASTELESS MILITARY JOKES
TRULY TASTELESS KENNEDY JOKES
TRULY TASTELESS BLONDE JOKES
TRULY TASTELESS SALESMAN JOKES
BLANCHE KNOTT'S BOOK OF TRULY TASTELESS ETIQUETTE
THE WORST OF TRULY TASTELESS JOKES (HARDCOVER)
THE TRULY TASTELESS JOKE-A-DATE BOOK

Truly Tasteless Disadvantaged White Male Jokes

Blanche Knott

St. Martin's Paperbacks

TRULY TASTELESS DISADVANTAGED WHITE MALE JOKES

ISBN: 0-312-96274-6

Printed in the United States of America

St. Martin's Paperbacks edition/August 1997

10 9 8 7 6 5 4 3 2 1

To Paul F.
disadvantaged, but enlightened

Author's Note

Remember how white guys used to have it all? Private clubs, grateful wives, great salaries and upward mobility, optional diaper duty, no worries about PMS or safe sex, not to mention a little *respect*?

Not anymore. Nowadays, thanks to sensitivity training, the economy, affirmative action, and uppity women, it's all a disadvantaged white male can do to hang on to a six-pack and a shred of self-esteem. For a final kick in the teeth, here's a joke book just for them, because after all, what's twelve inches long and white?

Nothing.

—B. K.

Contents

Sexually Inept White Males 1

Utterly Useless White Males 15

Completely Sex-Obsessed White Males 28

Intellectually Challenged White Males 31

Sadly Underendowed White Males 49

Rude and Crude White Males 64

White Males Who Are Inferior to Women 69

White Males Who Are Superior to Women 80

Hopelessly Naive White Males 85

Absurdly Self-Absorbed White Males 96

Completely Miscellaneous White Males 102

SEXUALLY INEPT WHITE MALES

A fellow met this girl and she seemed willing and he was dying to try, so even though they didn't know quite what to do, very soon they were doing it.

"If I'd known you were a virgin," the man said afterward, "I'd have taken my time."

"If I'd known you had time," she retorted, "I'd have taken off my panty hose."

•

Why is it ridiculous for women to complain that white men make love too fast?

How much speed can you build up in 45 seconds?

•

Joe was in the corner bar having a few when his friend Phil dropped in and joined him. It didn't take long for Phil to notice a string hanging out of the back of Joe's shirt collar that his friend kept tugging on.

Finally Phil couldn't contain his curiosity. "What the hell's that string for?" he asked.

"Two weeks ago I had a date with that dish, Linda," Joe explained, "and when I got her into the sack, would you believe I couldn't perform? Made me so mad that I tied this string on it, and every time I think of how it let me down, I pull the string and make it kiss my ass."

•

What's a WASP's idea of foreplay?

Drying the dishes.

•

How can you tell when your date suffers from premature ejaculation?

When he walks in the door.

•

This guy is out on a date with a girl and they end up back at his apartment on the couch with the lights off. Suddenly, to his horror, his hairpiece falls off and he begins to grope around in the dark for it.

Not realizing what's happened, his date begins cooing passionately. "That's it, honey," she whispers, "right there. You've got it . . . you've got it now. . . ."

"No I don't," he says, sitting up and looking at her. "My hairpiece isn't parted in the middle."

•

One day a young woman was walking home when a man grabbed her, dragged her into a back alley, and started molesting her. "Help! Help me, someone," she cried. "I'm being robbed!"

"You ain't being robbed, lady," interrupted the man, "you're being screwed."

"Well if this is being screwed," she said, "I'm being robbed."

•

How do you say "premature ejaculation" in French?

"Ooh la la—so soon?"

•

A man who had problems with premature ejaculation went to a sex shop for a remedy. The clerk handed him a little yellow can and said, "This is Stay-Hard Spray; put on a little and you can go all night!"

Delighted, the guy took it home, stowed it on the cellar shelf, and waited eagerly for bedtime, when he sprayed some on his dick and hustled upstairs. But to his disgust, he came quicker than ever. The next day he returned to the sex shop, slammed the can down on the counter, and snapped, "This stuff makes me worse than before!"

Reading the label, the clerk asked, "Did you hide this stuff on the cellar shelf?"

"Yeah, so?" said the disgruntled customer.

"You must have grabbed the wrong can. This is Easy-Off."

•

What does a woman say after her third orgasm?

You mean you don't know?

•

This guy went to a whorehouse and asked for Lila. The madam went to check if Lila was free, and returned to say that she was available, but that the cost was $150.

"Gee, that's pretty steep," complained the customer. "It was only 50 bucks last week."

"Take it or leave it," said the madam with a shrug, so he handed the money over and went up to Lila's room.

As he was getting dressed afterward, he asked the prostitute, "Well, how was I?"

"Absolutely the most inept fuck I've ever had, even for a white guy," replied the hooker, "just like I told you the last time you were here. You were *terrible.* Why do you think I tripled my fee? Why'd you come back here anyway?"

"Just wanted a second opinion," he explained cheerfully.

•

Why did God create the orgasm?

So women wouldn't have to wait for the second coming.

•

Marvin liked to hang out at the beach, and he couldn't help noticing this other guy who had girls all around him like bees around a flower. Finally Marvin went over to shoot the bull with the lifeguard. "Some guys have all the luck, eh?" he commented. "Just look at that one; you just know he's getting more pussy than any man can handle. How come I'm not making out like him?"

"You really want to know?" said the lifeguard with a grin. "The next time you come down to the beach, try putting a potato in your bathing suit."

This sounded like a good suggestion to Marvin, so he couldn't understand why everyone was cracking up when he took his next stroll in the surf. "Hey, man, I just followed your advice," he complained to the lifeguard. "How come everyone's laughing at me?"

The lifeguard leaned forward and whispered confidentially, "The potato's supposed to go in the *front* of your suit."

•

A couple of truck drivers met at a diner on an interstate. "Yo, Jack," said one to the other, "I haven't seen you in months. How're you doing? Getting any on the side?"

Jack sighed wearily and said, "I haven't had any in so long I didn't know they'd moved it."

•

While in the midst of a passionate embrace with a prostitute, the admiral asked, "Well, how'm I doing, mate?"

"Oh, I'd say you're doing about three knots," the hooker answered.

"What do you mean by three knots?" he asked with a leer and a pinch.

"You're not hard, you're not in, and you're not getting a refund."

•

The horny guy had just parked the car in lover's lane when his girlfriend announced that she wanted to break up with him. "Aw, honey," he sighed. "How could you do this to me? At least let me look at it once more."

Being a good-natured girl, she obliged, stepping out of the car and pulling up her skirt. It was a moonless night, however, and the boyfriend couldn't see a thing, so he struck a match and bent over for a closer look. "My God," he exclaimed, "can you pee through all that hair?"

"Of course," was the puzzled reply.

"Well you better, because it's on fire!"

•

The first astronaut to land on Mars was delighted to come across a beautiful Martian woman stirring a huge pot over a campfire. "Hi there," he said casually. "What're you doing?"

"Making babies," she explained, looking up with a winsome smile.

Horny after the long space voyage, the astronaut decided to give it a shot. "That's not the way we do it on Earth," he informed her.

"Oh, really?" The Martian woman looked up from her pot with interest. "How do your people do it?"

"Well, it's hard to describe," he conceded, "but I'd be glad to show you."

"Fine," agreed the lovely Martian maiden, and the two proceeded to make love in the glow of the fire. Whey they were finished, she asked, "So where are the babies?"

"Oh, they don't show up for another nine months," explained the astronaut patiently.

"So why'd you stop stirring?"

•

Why did the WASP think he'd hurt his girlfriend during sex?

She moved.

•

After a few years of marriage, the young woman became increasingly dismayed by her diminishing sex life. She tried everything she could think of, from greeting her husband at the door dressed in Saran Wrap layers to purchasing exotic paraphernalia from a mail-order sex boutique. But none of it had the desired effect on her husband's libido, and finally she persuaded him to consult a hypnotist.

She was delighted that after only a few visits, her husband's ardor was restored to honeymoon dimensions. There was only one annoying side effect: Every so often during lovemaking he would jump up and run out of the room for a minute or two. At first his wife didn't want to rock the boat, but eventually her curiosity overcame her better judgment. Following him into the bathroom, she saw him staring into the mirror, muttering, "She's not my wife. . . . She's not my wife. . . . She's not my wife. . . ."

•

Soon after their honeymoon, the young couple found themselves at the doctor's office, where each complained of exhaustion and fatigue. After examining them thoroughly, the doctor reassured them that there was no organic reason for their complaints.

"However, it's not at all uncommon for young people to wear themselves out in the first weeks or months of married life," he reassured them. "What you both need is rest. So for the next month, confine your sexual activity to those days of the week with an "R" in them. That's Thursday, Friday, and Saturday," he went on with a wink, "and you'll be feeling up to snuff very soon."

Since the end of the week was approaching, the couple had no problem following the doctor's advice. But on the first scheduled night off, the new bride found herself increasingly restless and horny. Tossing and turning into the wee hours, she finally turned to her husband and shook him awake.

Groggy and bewildered, he mumbled, "What's wrong, baby? What day is it?"

"Mondray," she murmured.

•

"I've been married three times and I'm still a virgin," complained Myrna to her new friend. "My first husband was a college professor; he only talked about it. My second husband was a doctor; he only looked at it. And my third husband was a gourmet."

•

Casey made an appointment with a sex therapist and explained that he and his wife were unable to achieve simultaneous climax. "It's not a terrible problem, Doctor," he conceded, "but isn't there something I could do about it?"

The therapist confided that he and his wife had had the same problem, which he'd solved by hiding a pistol under his pillow. "When I was about to come, I reached for the gun and fired a shot, and Doreen climaxed with me. Come back next week and tell me how it works for you."

That very night the therapist got a call from the county hospital and rushed over to the emergency room. "What happened, Casey?" he cried, catching sight of his patient writhing in pain on an examining table, clutching a bloodsoaked towel to his groin.

Wincing, Casey explained that he'd gone right out

to purchase a .45, hid it under the pillow, and started making love to his wife. "And when I was about to come, I grabbed the gun and fired."

"So?" pursued the doctor.

"She shat in my face and bit off the end of my dick."

•

Two old high-school friends got together for dinner one night. "I haven't gotten laid in months," moaned Brenda. "How's *your* sex life?"

"Oh, Paul and I do it all the time," answered Joelle, taking a bite of her salad, "but it kind of reminds me of an exercise bike."

"How come?"

"He gets on, he pumps and pumps, but we never seem to get anywhere."

•

What do you call a woman who moans and groans in ecstasy while having sex with her husband?

A hypocrite.

•

An international conference of sexologists was convened to determine once and for all why the penis is shaped the way it is. Each national delegation had done extensive research and was to present its results.

Said the Cuban spokesman, "We have spent five million pesos and can now state that the penis is definitely that shape in order to give pleasure to the woman."

"I beg to disagree," opined the Japanese representative. "We've spent millions of yen and are quite sure that the shape is such that maximum pleasure is felt by the man."

"We've spent a million bucks," drawled the American delegate, "and there's no doubt about it: It's that shape so your hand doesn't slip off the end."

•

How can a white male tell when he's had a really good orgasm?

His girlfriend wakes up.

•

Three friends were out enjoying a night on the town, and the suggestion that they visit the local whorehouse met with enthusiasm all around—especially when the madam told them there was a special offer that evening. For $100, $150, or $200, the customer would receive a sexual treat beyond his wildest dreams.

The first guy forks out $100, is shown to the first door on the right, and soon his friends hear cries of ecstasy coming from within. He emerges some time later, still sweaty and out of breath and grinning from ear to ear. "She's the most beautiful woman I've ever seen," he says happily, and goes on to explain that after extensive foreplay she had put two pineapple rings around his penis and eaten them.

The second guy can hardly wait to fork over his $150, is shown to a room, and soon wild cries of bliss can be heard. Eventually he returns with the same grin and the same story, except that he had gotten whipped cream along with the two pineapple rings.

The third guy needs little persuading to part with his $200 and is shown to an upstairs room. Soon cries of ecstasy can be heard, but his friends are puzzled when they're interrupted by a scream of agony. When he eventually returns, they can't wait to hear what happened. Yes, he explains wearily, she was the most beautiful woman he'd ever seen, and after extensive foreplay she had covered his prick with two pineapple rings, whipped cream, chopped nuts, and topped it off with a maraschino cherry.

"So then what happened?" ask his friends eagerly.

"Well," he replies, "it looked so good I ate it myself."

•

Boyfriend: "Wanna have a quickie?

Girlfriend: "As opposed to what?"

•

As a last resort, Mr. Jones went to a sex therapist, confiding that his sex life was abysmal. The doctor leaned back in his big leather chair and advised, "Have a few martinis first, to loosen things up a bit. Then let your mind roam over the possibilities; think about how exciting you used to find the whole business." They glanced out the office window into the courtyard, where two dogs happened to be screwing vigorously. "You see—just look at the vitality and vigor of those animals," the doctor exhorted happily. "Go home and reflect on their spontaneity over a few drinks. I'll see you in two weeks."

Two weeks later, the therapist asked, "Well? How'd it go?"

"Terribly," answered the patient glumly. "It took seven martinis just to get her out in the yard."

•

Being a virgin, Bob was very nervous about his upcoming wedding night, so he decided to seek the advice of his friend John, who was quite the local Romeo. "Just relax, Bob," counseled John. "After all, you grew up on a farm—just do like the dogs do."

Right after the honeymoon the bride stormed over to her mother's house in tears and announced that she wasn't going to live under the same roof as Bob for even one more night. "He's totally disgusting!" she wailed.

At first Bob's bride resisted her mother's attempts to find out the exact nature of the problem, but finally she broke down. "Ma, he doesn't know anything at all about how to be romantic, how to make love . . . he just keeps smelling my ass and pissing on the bedpost!"

•

What's red and has seven little dents in it?

Snow White's cherry.

•

Did you hear about the guy who went to a Premature Ejaculators Anonymous meeting but nobody was there?

He was an hour early.

UTTERLY USELESS WHITE MALES

Why did God invent men?
Because you can't get a vibrator to mow the lawn.

•

What's the difference between a new husband and a new dog?
After a year, the dog is still excited to see you.

•

What's the difference between government bonds and frat boys?
Bonds mature.

•

Why is masturbation better than having sex with a man?

You know who you're dealing with.
You don't have to wait till it's hard again.
You know when you've had enough.
And you don't have to lie about how good it was.

•

What's the function of a man?
Life-support system for a penis.

•

How is being at a singles bar different from going to the circus?
At the circus the clowns don't talk.

•

An inquisitive young man was on a flight to Hawaii and was having a number of drinks to help get him in the vacation spirit. Quite perturbed to discover that the men's room was under repair, he asked the stewardess for admittance to the ladies' room.

"Certainly," said the stewardess graciously, "as long as you don't touch the buttons marked WW, PP, and ATR."

Rather desperate, the young man readily agreed, but no sooner had he relieved himself than his curiosity got the better of him. Pressing the WW button, he enjoyed the sensation of warm water being sprayed up onto his rear end. This was so pleasant that he barely hesitated before depressing the PP button, and was rewarded by the soft pat of a powder puff on his bottom. Much emboldened, he pushed the button marked ATR.

He felt a searing pain, and the next thing he knew, he was waking up in a bright, white room with a nurse standing by his bedside.

"You pushed the WW button, right?" she asked with a knowing look in her eye.

"Yes," the young man admitted.

"And the PP button?"

The man nodded.

"And then you pushed the ATR button, am I correct?"

"Yeah, so?"

"ATR stands for Automatic Tampon Removal," explained the nurse. "By the way, your penis is on your pillow."

•

Did you hear about the white guy who was so inept he got fired?

From Amway.

•

How many men does it take to change a roll of toilet paper?

We don't know—it's never happened.

•

What makes a white guy think he's so great?

—He has a bellybutton that won't work.
—He has tits that won't give milk.
—He has a cock that won't crow.
—He has balls that won't roll.
—And an ass that won't carry a thing.

•

What's a white guy's cure for boredom?

Drinking a whole bottle of Ex-Lax so he'll have something to do.

•

"Say," said Lucille one day over lunch, "weren't you going to go out with that guy who played the French horn?"

"Yeah," said Diane, stirring her ice tea.

"You were really looking forward to it, I remember. How'd it go?" Lucille leaned forward eagerly.

"Actually he was a pretty nice guy," volunteered Diane reluctantly. "But there was one real problem . . ."

"Oh, really?"

"Every time he kissed me, he wanted to shove his fist up my ass."

•

What can Life Savers do that a man can't?

Come in five different flavors.

•

Did you hear about the really dumb white guy whose family kept telling him he'd never get into medical school?

He finally did—as a cadaver.

•

What's the advantage of firing a redneck?

You won't have to hire a replacement.

•

What's an ideal husband?

A guy with a three-million-dollar insurance policy who dies on the wedding night.

•

What do you sit on that's long and hard, has four letters, begins with "D" and ends with "K"?

A dock.

•

What's the lawyer's definition of a bachelor?

Some son of a bitch who's cheated a deserving woman out of her divorce settlement.

•

What did the white guy do when the girl whispered, "What I want is a man who'll really deliver."

Ran out for a pizza.

Orville went to specialist after specialist in search of a diagnosis, and it finally emerged that he was suffering from a rare enzymatic disorder, the only treatment for which was fresh breast milk. So he advertised in the want ads for a wet nurse, and was delighted when a woman promptly responded. Explaining the situation over the phone, he negotiated a fee and made an appointment for the next day.

It so happened that Orville had always been a tit man and had an exceptionally skilled set of lips and tongue, and that after a few minutes the woman found herself extremely aroused. Squirming, and breathing heavily, she managed to gasp, "Uh . . . is there anything else I could offer you?"

"Mmm," murmured Orville, looking up and wiping his chin. "You don't happen to have any Oreos, do you?"

•

How do you know if a white guy's a loser?

If the only way he gets to see a woman naked is by buying the clothes off a store mannequin.

•

How can you tell if he's a *real* loser?

He only wakes up stiff if he jogged ten miles the day before.

•

Two women were comparing notes on their husbands. "Irving is just impossible," sighed the first one. "He's just impossible to please. How about your Milton, is he hard to please?"

"I don't know," replied the other woman with a shrug. "I've never tried."

•

What's a cheap guy's idea of a royal evening out?

Dinner at Burger King and dessert at Dairy Queen.

•

The horny midget found that the best way to make time with women was to be direct about it. So he went up to the tallest, blondest woman at the party and said, "Hey, honey, whaddaya say to a little fuck?"

She looked down at him and replied, "Hello, you little fuck!"

•

Mike came home from work a little depressed one day. "Honey," he asked his wife over dinner, "suppose I had a horrible accident and was crippled or something. Would you still love me?"

"Of course, darling," she assured him. "I'll always love you."

"How about if I became impotent and couldn't make love to you anymore?" he continued.

"Don't worry, honey, I'll always love you."

"Say I lost my job as executive vice president and wasn't pulling in six figures anymore?" he pressed anxiously.

"Like I said, Mike, I'll always love you," she replied coolly, "and I'll really miss you, too."

•

Why do women have more trouble than men with hemorrhoids?

Because when God created man, He created the perfect asshole.

•

How does a man show he's planning for the future?

He buys two cases of beer instead of one.

•

One morning old Pa Jones informed his ancient wife that he was planning a trip into town that day to apply for Social Security. "But, Pa," she pointed out, "you don't have a birth certificate. How're you going to prove your age?"

"Now don't you worry, Ma." Giving her a little pat, Pa headed out. Sure enough he was back in a few hours with the news that the first check would be along within three weeks.

"So how'd you prove your age, eh?" asked his wife.

"Easy," said Pa with a smile. "I just unbuttoned my shirt and showed 'em all the gray hairs on my chest."

"Well while you were at it," scolded the old woman, "why didn't you drop your pants and apply for disability?"

•

What do you do with a bachelor who thinks he's God's gift?

Exchange him.

•

Why are husbands like lawn mowers?

They're hard to get started, emit foul odors, and don't work half the time.

•

Dorman graduated from an Ivy League university and went on to get a Ph.D. in mechanical engineering, only to find out there wasn't a job in town for which his qualifications applied. After months of job-hunting, he was desperate enough to answer a tiny "Help Wanted" ad. The job turned out to be a whorehouse, where the proprietor explained, "I need someone to collect the dirty sheets and sweep up at the end of the night."

"Lady, you don't understand," protested Dorman. "I'm a Phi Beta Kappa with a doctorate in engineering."

"Okay, okay," said the woman with a sigh. "I'll show you how."

•

What are the five worst things about being a penis?

1) You have a hole in your head.
2) You have permanent ring-around-the-collar.
3) Your next-door neighbors are two nuts and an ass-hole.
4) Your best friend is a cunt.
5) And every time you get excited, you throw up.

•

How can you tell when your husband is really ugly?

When you go to a mate-swapping party and you have to throw in the mailman.

•

A well-dressed man walked into a nice bar. Ordering two martinis, he drank one down and proceeded to pour the second on his hand. Unable to contain his curiosity, the bartender leaned over. "I hope you don't mind me asking, sir, but why'd you just waste a good drink?"

The man explained, "I just want to get my date drunk."

•

What's a white guy's cue that his partner is losing interest?
When her favorite sexual position is "next door."

•

How can you tell a dumb man designed the lower half of a woman's anatomy?
Who else would put the snack bar so close to the shithole?

•

What's the difference between a man and a computer?
After five years, you can still count on the computer to go down on you every so often.

•

Why don't men have midlife crises?
They stay stuck in adolescence.

•

"When my wife climaxes," the man complained to the marriage counselor, "she lets out this earsplitting yell."
"All things considered," commented the counselor, "I'd think that might be a source of some satisfaction for you."
"Oh, it would be," he said, "if it didn't wake me up."

•

Did you hear about the white guy who finally got a blind date?

He put sunglasses on his inflatable sex doll.

•

The gynecologist stuck up his head after completing his examination. "I'm sorry," he reported, "but I'm going to have to remove that vibrator surgically if you're going to be able to have sexual intercourse again."

"It's not worth it," sighed the woman on the examining table. "Why don't you just replace the batteries?"

•

Why do men have bigger brains than dogs?

So they don't hump women's legs at cocktail parties.

•

How can you tell a guy's a real loser?

When he calls a porn service and the girl says, "Not tonight, I've got an earache."

•

What's another way?

When you go to a diner and people drop change in his coffee cup.

•

What do you call the useless piece of flesh at the end of a penis?
A man.

COMPLETELY SEX-OBSESSED WHITE MALES

Hear about the little white kid whose mother caught him jerking off in the bathroom?

She told him to stop because he'd go blind and he asked if he could keep going till he needed glasses.

•

What makes men chase women they have no intention of marrying?

The same urge that makes dogs chase cars they have no intention of driving.

•

What's an insecure lover's idea of fantasizing during sex?

Imagining he's someone else.

•

Jake and Jim were about to head out for another long winter trapping in the northernmost wilds of Saskatchewan. When they stopped for provisions at the last tiny town, the proprietor of the general store, knowing it was going to be a good many months without female companionship, offered them two boards featuring fur-lined holes.

"We won't be needing anything like that," Jim protested, and Jake shook his head righteously. But the storekeeper pressed the boards on them, pointing out that they could always be burned as firewood.

Seven months later, bearded and gaunt, Jake walked into the general store. After a little chitchat about the weather and the trapping, the storekeeper asked where his partner was.

"I shot the son of a bitch," snarled Jake. "Caught him trying to date my board."

•

How was Colonel Sanders a typical male?

All he cared about were legs, breasts, and thighs.

•

Ira runs into an old friend on the golf course one Sunday morning and proudly announces that he and his wife are about to have triplets. "Pretty amazing, huh? And you know, they say triplets only occur once in 185,000 times."

"Is that so?" His friend is truly impressed. "How the hell do you find the time for golf?"

•

Why do men find it difficult to make eye contact?
Breasts don't have eyes.

•

The only survivor of a shipwreck, Pierre washed ashore on a desert island. He managed to find food and water, and didn't mind the solitude, but he grew horny as hell, so when a sheep walked down the beach one day, he jumped at it. Pierre led the beast back to his hut, but just as he was starting to get it on, a dog ran out of the jungle and began to attack him. And in trying to beat the dog away, Pierre had to let the sheep go.

In the weeks that followed the sheep appeared regularly, but every time Pierre tried to get romantic with her, the dog materialized and attacked him viciously.

A few months later a lovely young woman washed up on the shore. She was half drowned, but Pierre was able to resuscitate her, and when she came to, she was grateful beyond words. "You saved my life," she sobbed. "I would have drowned. How may I repay you? I'll do anything, just name it . . . Anything!"

Pierre grabbed the sheep and ordered, "Hold that dog."

•

How many men does it take to screw in a lightbulb?
One. Men will screw anything.

INTELLECTUALLY CHALLENGED WHITE MALES

When Mitch walked into the corner bar late one night he was obviously steaming mad. He downed three shots before a friend came over and asked what was wrong.

"It's my wife, I can't believe it. When I got home tonight she was lying in bed all hot and bothered, and it made me suspicious. So I looked around, and sure enough, there was a naked guy hiding behind the shower curtain, can you beat it?"

"Jesus. No wonder you're so pissed off," said his buddy sympathetically.

"Yeah, but that's not all," the furious husband continued. "That son of a bitch in the shower, he lied his way out of it."

•

Why are blonde jokes so short?

So white guys can remember them.

•

Two very nervous young men got to talking in the doctor's waiting room and discovered they had similar symptoms: One had a red ring around the base of his penis and the other one a green ring. The fellow with the red ring was examined first. In a few minutes he came out, all smiles, and said, "Don't worry, man, it's nothing!"

Vastly relieved, the second patient went in to the examining room, only to be told a few minutes later by the doctor, "I'm very sorry, but you have an advanced case of V.D. and your penis will have to be amputated."

Turning white as a sheet, the young man gasped, "But the first guy . . . he said it was no big deal!"

"Well, you know," said the doctor, "there's a big difference between gangrene and lipstick."

•

Judy was in bed with her lover when her husband came home unexpectedly early. "What the hell are you doing!" he cried when he came through the bedroom door.

"See?" said Judy to her boyfriend, "Didn't I tell you he was incredibly stupid?"

•

What do men and beer bottles have in common?

They're both empty from the neck up.

•

Keith was having dinner by himself one night when he realized that a good-looking woman kept looking over at him from across the room. Finally, as he was paying his bill, she came over and said, "I'm not usually this blunt, but I'm really attracted to you. How about giving me your phone number?"

"No problem, it's in the phone book," replied Keith.

"Okay, so what's your name?" she asked.

"Oh, that's in the phone book too."

•

Why did the inept speculator feed nylon to his chickens?

He wanted them to lay L'Eggs.

•

Did you hear about the dumb white guy who was so strapped for cash he held up a lawyer?

He lost $1,100.

•

One summer evening in New York a girl strolling across Broadway was hit by a truck. The impact was so strong that she flew up into the air, and by the time she hit the ground all her clothes had been stripped away.

As a crowd started to gather, a passing priest who had witnessed the accident rushed over and placed his hat over the victim's crotch so as to preserve a little decency.

Soon a drunkard, wondering what was going on, staggered through the crowd and caught sight of the naked girl lying in the street, covered only by the priest's hat. "Oh Christ," he mumbled, "first thing we have to do is get that man out of there."

•

What's the definition of "dumb"?

A guy who rolls up his sleeve when a girl says she wants to feel his muscle.

•

It was late in the day when the redneck shuffled into the police station and said he wanted to report a missing person.

"Tell me what happened," instructed the desk sergeant.

So Hiram explained that he and his wife of 40 years were out taking an afternoon stroll alone Route 12 when a huge truck came barreling along the road. "So I jumps off the road and lets the damn truck go on by . . . but then I can't see Tanya anywhere."

"She probably got so scared that she turned right around and went home," suggested the sergeant.

"Well . . . maybe," conceded the old man reluctantly. "But I keeps walking along the road, and first I see Tanya's handbag hanging from the branch of a hawthorn tree. Little ways up, I sees her arm in the ditch. Not ten feet farther on, there's her left leg by the side of the road. So after a while I get to thinking maybe something's happened to Tanya."

•

What did the white teenager do with the pound of cocaine?

Snorted a gram and sold the rest to a narc.

•

When the extremely obese man showed up for his doctor's appointment, he claimed he'd tried every possible way to lose weight. So the doctor proposed a radical diet: rectal feeding. Reassuring his patient that he wouldn't starve to death, the doctor explained that adequate nutrients would be absorbed through the rectal walls, and that weight loss was virtually guaranteed.

A month later the patient came in for his follow-up appointment; sure enough, he's down from 360 to a trim 175 pounds. Showing him into his office and observing that the onetime fatty was bouncing up and down in his seat energetically, the doctor asked how he was feeling. "Just fine, Doc, never better," was the cheerful reply.

"Well then why are you bouncing up and down like that?" asked the puzzled doctor.

"Just chewing some gum!"

•

Did you hear about the white guy who invited a woman out to dinner and had sex that very night?

He took her home and jerked off half an hour later.

•

How about the one who waited until he was 64 to make love to his wife?

He'd read that most couples have sex just before retiring.

•

Schenck brings his friend Shrafft home from work with him early one day. They come upstairs to find his wife, and there she is in bed with another man.

Schenck turns calmly away from the doorway and says to Shrafft, "Let's go downstairs and have a cup of coffee."

"Uh, okay," agrees his friend, so they sit around the kitchen for the longest time, until finally Shrafft can't stand it anymore. "Schenck," he blurts, "what about the guy upstairs?"

"Fuck him," says Schenck. "Let him make his own goddamn coffee."

•

The cowhand got paid on Friday and immediately rode into town and proceeded to get thoroughly shitfaced. Observing his condition, a couple of pals decided to play a trick on him. They sneaked out of the saloon, turned his horse around, turned the saddle around too, and went back to join the hapless drunk for a few more rounds.

The next morning, when the alarm clock and a glass of cold water in his face failed to have the slightest effect, the cowhand's wife started shaking him by the shoulders and screaming, "Tex, get up! You have to hit the goddamn trail, you've got work to do."

"Can't," mumbled Tex. "Too beat. Too tired. Can't even lift my head."

"Get the hell up!" she screamed in his ear. "I've seen you this hungover a thousand times."

"Last night was different," said the wretched fellow. "Some son of a bitch cut my horse's head off, and I had to pull him all the way home with my finger in his windpipe!"

•

Why didn't the cracker's dogs do tricks?

You have to be smarter than the dog to teach it stuff.

•

How did the earnest white guy prepare for his vacation in Switzerland?

He decided to take Swiss lessons.

•

Bill was pretty naive when it came to sex, so he decided to take matters into his own hands and pay a visit to the local prostitute. But no sooner had he been shown into her room and taken down his pants, than he shot his wad.

"Too bad, sonny," commiserated the hooker. "Can you come again?"

"Oh, no problem," Bill replied happily. "I live right in the neighborhood."

•

What did the Georgia politician say when they asked him to spell Mississippi?

"The state or the river?"

•

What are a woman's three most successful lies?

1) You're the best.
2) You're the biggest.
3) It doesn't always smell that way.

•

A lot of men know what they want. . . .

They just can't spell it.

•

Bert had just turned 50 and became concerned that his stamina in bed was really declining. So he went to consult his doctor, who pointed out that his general physical condition left something to be desired. "You're a little overweight, you're easily winded, you're just out of shape. I recommend jogging five miles a day," said the doctor. "It'll really improve your stamina in general." And though Bert was a couch potato by nature, he reluctantly agreed to the regimen.

A week later, the doctor's phone rang. "Hi Bert, how're you feeling?" asked the medic.

"Really terrific," enthused his patient.

"And how's your sex life?"

"What sex life?" countered Bert. "I'm 35 miles from home."

•

Why wouldn't the dumb Aggie sign the million-dollar pro ball contract?

He insisted on Sundays off.

•

It was a hot summer Saturday, and a bunch of little kids were sitting out on the porch stoop with no money, nowhere to go, nothing to do. Finally Spencer's father stuck his head out the window, tossed his kid five bucks, and told the kids to get lost.

Spencer dashed off down the street on his bike, the others following after him, and they were very surprised when he disappeared into the corner drugstore. In a few minutes he emerged carrying a small brown bag. "What's in the bag?" clamored his friends, crowding around him eagerly.

They were less than pleased when he pulled out a box of Tampax tampons. "Hey, man," they groaned collectively, "we wanted to go out and buy ourselves a good time with that money. What'd you go and buy *that* for?"

"That's why I *got* it," Spencer explained with a big smile. "It says right here on the box: You can go swimming, you can go horseback riding. . . ."

•

What did the dumb man do before going to the cockfight?

Greased his zipper.

•

Fleming was arrested for peeing in the park and was brought before the judge. "Since this is your first offense, I'll go easy on you," said the judge, "but I'm trusting that we won't see any further such disgraceful and unseemly behavior from you. The fine will be $25."

"Gee, thanks, Your Honor," the defendant responded. He handed the judge a $50 bill and headed out of the courtroom.

"Hold on a second, Mr. Fleming," called the judge. You forgot your change."

"You might as well hang onto it," Fleming called out cheerfully from the back of the room. "I'm pretty sure I can hit your water cooler from here."

•

What does a man get if he crosses a hooker with a pit bull?

His last blow job.

•

Did you hear about the Okie who finished his first book?

Reading it, that is.

•

When dim-witted Jack came home from a business trip a day early, his worst fears were confirmed: He found his wife in bed with his best friend Mick. She screamed, Mick dove for his clothes, and Jack reached into the bureau drawer and pulled out a gun. But when he pointed it at his own temple, she couldn't help bursting out laughing.

"Don't feel sorry for me, you heartless bitch," roared the cuckold. "You're next!"

•

Myron hadn't been feeling too well, so he went to his doctor for a checkup. After a thorough examination, the doctor sat him down and said gravely, "I'm afraid I have two pieces of very bad news for you, Myron."

"What bad news?" he gasped.

"You have AIDS," replied the doctor, "and as of this date, there is no known cure."

Myron slumped in his chair, ashen-faced. After composing himself for a few minutes, he asked quietly for the other piece of bad news.

"You also have Alzheimer's disease," responded the physician, "and that's incurable, too."

Again Myron sat silently for a few minutes. Then, his face brightening, he pointed out, "Well, it could be worse. At least I don't have AIDS."

•

Ron went off on a long business trip, and took a day off before returning to the office. Over lunch the next day, he confessed sheepishly to his buddies that he'd been taking for granted how much his wife loved him.

"Yeah? How come?" asked a co-worker.

"She was *so* happy to have me back home," he reported with a grin, "that every time the doorbell rang, whether it was the mailman, or the UPS guy, or our neighbor Rick, she'd yell, 'Ron's home! My husband's home!' "

•

Gina fell for her handsome new dentist like a ton of bricks, and pretty soon had lured him into a series of passionate encounters in the dental clinic after hours. But one day he said sadly, "Gina, we've got to stop seeing each other. Your husband's bound to get suspicious."

"No way, sweetheart, he's dumb as a post," Gina assured him. "Besides, we've been screwing for six months now and he doesn't suspect a thing."

"True," agreed the dentist, "but you're down to one tooth."

•

When Ernie walked into the pharmacy and asked for rubbers, the girls behind the counter asked politely, "What size, please?"

"Gee, I don't know," answered Ernie, a little flustered, so she instructed him to use the fence out back to determine the correct size. And as he walked out the back door, she ran out a side door, around, and behind the fence.

The fence had three holes in it.

Putting his penis in the first hole, Ernie felt capable hands gently stroking it. Reluctantly, he pulled it out and inserted it in the second hole, and within seconds, he felt a warm, wet pussy at work on the other side of the fence. Groaning with pleasure, he managed to pull out and stick it through the third hole. There he felt an expert set of lips and tongue give him the blow job of his dreams.

Leaving her customer groaning in ecstasy, the girl jumped up and hurried behind the counter. She was standing there with a smile when Ernie staggered back through the door.

"Your size, sir?" she asked politely.

"Forget the rubbers," he grunted. "Just gimme three yards of that fence."

•

Did you hear about the man who couldn't spell?

He spent the night in a warehouse.

•

Davey and Danny had been friends since kindergarten, and remained inseparable throughout their childhood. And when Davey finally decided to get married, the old friends were determined to make a night of it.

At the reception the booze flowed like water, the band played on, and it was well past midnight when Davey realized he hadn't seen his wife or his best friend for quite some time. Staggering around, he finally found his bride and his best friend energetically screwing on a couch upstairs. The groom gazed at the oblivious couple for a few moments, and then burst into laughter so hysterical that the noise brought several members of his family running.

Taking in the scene, his father asked, "What the hell's so goddamn funny?"

"That Danny," said Davey, wiping the tears of laughter off his cheek, "he's so drunk he thinks he's me."

•

Man: "Hi! Want to go out tonight?"

Woman: "No thanks, I'm on the rag."

Man: "That's okay, I'm in jeans myself."

•

What made the hockey player suspicious when his girlfriend told him she wanted to have sex in the back seat?

She was insisting he drive.

•

The traveling salesman checked into a futuristic motel. Realizing he needed a trim before tomorrow's big meeting, he called down to the desk clerk to ask if there was a barber on the premises. "I'm afraid not, sir," the clerk told him apologetically, "but down the hall is a vending machine that should serve your purposes."

Skeptical but intrigued, the salesman located the appropriate machine, inserted fifty cents, and stuck his head in the opening, at which the machine started to buzz and whir. Fifteen seconds later the salesman pulled out his head, surveyed his reflection, and discovered the best haircut of his life.

Two feet away was another machine with a sign that read, MANICURES—25 cents. "Why not?" thought the salesman. He paid the money, inserted his hands into the slot, and pulled them out perfectly manicured.

The next machine had a huge sign that read THIS MACHINE PROVIDES WHAT MEN NEED MOST WHEN AWAY FROM THEIR WIVES—50 cents. The salesman looked both ways, put in fifty cents, unzipped his fly, and stuck his dick into the machine. When it started buzzing, the guy let out a shriek of agony. Fifteen seconds later the machine shut off and, with trembling hands, he was able to withdraw his penis . . . now with a button sewed to the tip.

•

What did the white guy do when the prostitute asked him if wanted to have some fun?

Took her bowling.

•

Roy was extolling the virtues of his new girlfriend. In fact, she was so perfect in every way that he'd asked her to marry him—and she'd accepted. Why, he was the luckiest man in the entire universe.

"I'm really happy for you, Roy," his best friend assured him. "And what did you say this paragon's name is?"

"Betty Jo," replied Roy, a look of pure happiness coming over his face at the mere mention of her name. "Betty Jo Bronowski."

"Not Betty Jo Bronowski!" yelled his buddy. "Roy, you can't be serious about marrying her. She's slept with every man in Poughkeepsie!"

A frown passed over Roy's face as he reflected briefly. "Heck," he responded, "Poughkeepsie's not such a big town."

•

How did Captain Hook die?

Jock itch.

•

The newly engaged couple was necking in his car and things started getting pretty steamy. "Oh darling, darling," the girl gasped at last. "Kiss me where it smells."

So he drove her to New Jersey.

•

How did the clueless guy remember he'd eaten pussy the night before?
When he woke up in the morning and saw that his face looked like a glazed doughnut.

•

Did you hear about the man who was so dumb that he thought his wife had been to church when she came home with a Gideon's Bible?

•

What's a WASP's definition of communication problems?
When his girlfriend won't tell him who she's dating.

•

Did you hear about the woman who blamed her divorce on her obtuse husband's calculating mind?
He finally put two and two together.

•

The farm boy got hitched, and he couldn't wait to tell his best friend about the wedding night. "Boy is Lucille dumb," he chortled. "She put a pillow under her ass instead of her head!"

•

The carpenter got careless with the table saw one day, and the next thing he knew, all eight fingers were sliced right off. He rushed over to the emergency room, where the doctor inspected his mutilated hands. "Could be worse," he said encouragingly. "The cuts are nice and clean, and microsurgery's gotten so sophisticated that we'll be able to sew your hands right back together again. Give me the fingers."

"I don't have 'em."

"You don't have them!" howled the doctor. "You mean you just left them lying on the ground? How stupid can you be?"

"Now cool your jets, Doc, and tell me one thing," said the guy testily. "How was I gonna pick 'em up?"

SADLY UNDERENDOWED WHITE MALES

What does the perfect male look like?
Long, dark, and handsome.
(See what I mean about disadvantaged?)

•

"Why do you iron your bra when you have nothing to put into it?" asked the husband snidely.
"I iron your shorts, don't I?" retorted the wife.

•

One day Gary went into the local tattoo parlor with a somewhat odd request. He had this great new girlfriend named Wendy, he explained, and while their sex life was dynamite, he was sure it would be even better if he had her name tattooed on his prick.

The tattoo artist did her best to dissuade him, pointing out that it would be very painful, and that most of the time the tattoo would just read "Wy" anyway. But

Gary was undeterred, and went ahead with the tattoo. Sure enough, Wendy was crazy about the tattoo, and their sex grew even wilder and more frequent. Gary was a happy man.

One day he was downtown and had to take a leak in a public bathroom. At the next urinal was a big black guy, and when Gary looked over he was surprised to see "Wy" on this guy's penis as well. "How about that!" he exclaimed. "Say, is your girlfriend's name Wendy, too?"

"Dream on," answered the black guy. "Mine says, 'Welcome to Jamaica and Have a Nice Day.' "

•

There was this guy who desperately wanted to have sex with his girlfriend. However, he was too embarrassed because of his extremely small penis. So one night, he took her to a dark place where she couldn't see it and after furiously making out with her, dropped his pants and put his penis in her hand.

"Sorry, I don't smoke," she whispered.

•

What did the fainthearted flasher say to the woman in December?

"It's so cold—should I just describe myself?"

•

Why do men shake their cocks after they piss?

Because they can't train them to go SNIFF.

•

Sam the butcher desperately wanted to try to impress a beautiful lady customer, so one morning when she walked in he said, "Good morning, what can I do for you this lovely day?"

The woman replied sternly, "Give me some of that prime rib that's on special."

Sam shuffled around behind the counter. "It's been a long time since you've been by the shop," he said, the eagerness mounting in his voice, "so today, I'll do something special for you; I won't put my thumb on the scale!"

"Sam, dear," she replied coolly, "if your dick were as big as that thumb, I'd buy my meat here all the time."

•

Heard the new Webster's definition of "small"?

"Is it in yet?"

•

The patient cleared his throat a little embarrassedly before explaining his rather unusual problem. "YOU SEE, DOC," he boomed in a voice so deep and raspy it was almost impossible to understand, "I CAN'T GO ON WITH THIS VOICE ANYMORE—IT'S DRIVING ME CRAZY. CAN YOU FIX IT SO I SOUND LIKE A NORMAL PERSON?"

"I'll certainly try," said the doctor. After examining

the patient, he reported that some sort of weight was pulling on the vocal cords and distorting the voice. "Any idea what it could be?" he queried.

The patient cleared his throat again. "ACTUALLY DOC, I HAPPEN TO BE . . . UH . . . ESPECIALLY WELL ENDOWED, AND MAYBE THAT'S WHAT'S DOING IT. LISTEN, IF YOU HAVE TO REMOVE SOME OF IT, THAT'S FINE BY ME. I'LL DO *ANYTHING* TO GET A VOICE LIKE A REGULAR GUY." So the doctor went ahead and performed the operation.

Two weeks later the patient telephoned the doctor's office. "Hey Doc," he babbled happily, "I can't thank you enough. Finally I sound like anyone else—it's just great! After a pause, he asked, "Say, by the way, what'd you do with the piece of my penis you removed?"

"I THREW IT AWAY," said the doctor.

•

Hungry for company, the young couple is delighted when a spaceship lands on their very isolated farm and out steps a young, very humanoid, Martian couple. They get to talking and soon the wife invites the Martians to dinner. And over dinner the conversation is so stimulating and all four get along so well that they decide to swap partners for the night.

The farmer's wife and the male Martian get the master bedroom, and when he undresses she sees that his phallus is very small indeed. "What are you going to do with that?" she can't resist asking.

"Watch," he says smartly. He twists his right ear and his penis suddenly grows to 18 inches in length—but it's still as skinny as a pencil. And again the farmer's wife can't suppress a disparaging comment.

So the Martian twists his left ear, at which his prick grows thick as a sausage. And he and the woman proceed to screw like crazy all night long.

The next morning the Martian couple takes off after cordial farewells, and the farmer turns to his wife. "So how was it?" he asks curiously.

"It was fabulous, really out of this world," reports the wife with a big smile. "How about you?"

"Nothing special," admitted the farmer. "Kinda weird in fact. All night long she kept playing with my ears."

•

After Marty's and Mindy's marriage ended in a particularly bitter divorce, Mindy remarried within six months. Not long afterward she ran into her ex-husband at a local restaurant where she was having lunch with a girlfriend.

"So," said Marty, sidling up to their table, "how's your new husband?"

"Just fine, thanks," answered Mindy calmly.

"And how does he like your old, tired, worn-out pussy?" inquired Marty with a sneer.

"Oh, he likes it just fine," Mindy said cheerfully, "since he didn't have any trouble getting past the old, worn-out part."

•

Harry stopped by the funeral parlor to see his friend Joe, who was an embalmer, and found him at work on a corpse with a gigantic penis. The man's apparatus was so spectacular that Harry blurted out, "Wouldn't I love to have that cock!"

"You might as well—this guy doesn't need it anymore," said Joe, and he proceeded to cut off the organ and hand it to Harry. Harry wrapped it up carefully and took it home, where he found his wife in the kitchen making dinner. Deciding to have a little fun, Harry unwrapped the package, stuck it between his legs, and rushed into the kitchen, shouting, "Look, honey, look!"

His wife glanced over and asked, "What happened to Sidney?"

•

"Did you know your long, pointed belt buckle is a phallic symbol?" asked the psychologist, coming over to sit next to his attractive female patient on the couch.

"Huh-uh," replied his patient. "What's a phallic symbol?"

"Let me show you," offered the doctor eagerly, unzipping his fly.

"Oh, I get it—like a dick, only smaller."

•

The unemployed porno star was looking for someone to represent him. "Do you have an eight-by-ten?" asked an agent.

"Shit," said the actor, "if I had an eight-by-ten, I wouldn't be out of work."

•

Swallowing his pride, Fred finally made an appointment with the great foreign specialist and told him he wanted his penis enlarged. After examining him, the doctor prescribed a bottle of pills. "Each time you take one, say 'Wee,' " the doctor instructed him solemnly, "and your penis will actually grow."

Fred was barely out of the parking lot before he popped ten of the pills. Unfortunately he was so excited that he lost control of the car, and as it plunged over a cliff his squeal of terror—"Weeeeeeeeeeeeeee"—was heard loud and clear.

Not long afterward a couple was driving down the same road. "Look, honey," observed the woman, "there's the hairiest telephone pole I've ever seen."

•

There once was a bodybuilder who had to take a wicked piss, so he knocked a couple of people over on the way to the bathroom. When he finally got there, both urinals were occupied, so he tossed the nearest offender out the window. With a sigh of relief he quickly unzipped his fly, pulled out his nine-inch penis, and began to urinate. Turning to the guy next to him with a smile, he said, "Whew, I just made it."

Frankly impressed, his neighbor said, "Wow—will you make me one, too?"

•

"Doctor," the man told his physician, "I need a new penis."

The doctor took the request completely in stride. "No problem," he told his patient. "We have a five-incher, a seven-and-a-half-inch model, and a nine-incher. Which do you think would be right for you?"

"The nine-incher," the man decided on the spot. "But would it be possible to take a look at it first?"

"Of course," said the doctor obligingly.

"Gee, Doctor," asked the patient after a few moments, "could I have it in white?"

•

[Note: for this joke you need a long-necked beer bottle as a prop.]

A young woman was out on a date and couldn't seem to come up with anything to talk about but her old boyfriend—his hobbies, his car, his habits. [Stroke the length of the bottle lovingly during this part of the joke.]

Finally the new man in her life grew exasperated. "You're always going on about him!" he exploded. "How about thinking about *me* for a change."

"You've got a point," she admitted. [Move your hand up to stroke just the neck of the bottle.] "I'll try."

•

Jack was delighted by the opportunity to use the golf course at the swank country club, and even more so when he hit a hole in one on the eighth hole. As he bent over to take his ball out of the cup, a genie popped out. "This club is so exclusive that my magical services are available to anyone who hits a hole in one on this hole," the genie explained. "Any wish you desire shall be granted."

"How about that!" Jack was thrilled, and immediately requested a longer penis.

"Your wish is granted," intoned the genie solemnly, and disappeared down the hole in a puff of incense.

The golfer went on down the green, and as he walked, he could feel his dick slowly lengthening. As the game progressed, Jack could feel it growing and growing, down his thigh, out from his shorts leg, down past his knee. "Maybe this wasn't such a great plan after all," muttered Jack to himself, and headed back to the eighth hole with a bucket of balls. Finally he managed a hole in one, and when he went to collect the ball, he had to hold up the head of his penis to keep it from dragging on the ground.

Out popped the genie. "This club is so exclusive that my magical services are available to anyone who hits a hole in one on this hole. Any wish you—"

"Yeah, yeah, yeah," interrupted Jack. "Could you make my legs longer?"

•

Joe and Moe went outside to take a leak and Joe confessed, "I wish I had one like my cousin Junior. He needs four fingers to hold his."

Moe looked over and pointed out, "But you're holding *yours* with four fingers."

"I know," said Joe with a sigh, "but I'm peeing on three of them."

•

What was the white guy's clue that his penis was really small?

When his girlfriend went down on him, she didn't suck, she flossed.

•

The Bergs went over to the local Oldsmobile dealership to pick out a new car. No sooner had gorgeous Mrs. Berg set foot on the car lot than the salesman's jaw dropped. He couldn't take his eyes off her.

Never one to pass up a chance at a bargain, Berg pulled the salesman aside. "She's really something, eh?" he commented with a sly smile.

The salesman nodded dumbly, eyes glued to Mrs. Berg's cleavage.

"Tell you what," Berg proposed. "You've got a back room here, right? Let's take her back there, and if you can do everything I can do, I'll pay double the price of the best car on the lot. If you can't, I get it half-price."

The salesman agreed enthusiastically, his gaze dropping to Mrs. Berg's perfect, miniskirted ass. As soon as the door was closed, Berg pulled up his wife's T-shirt and started fondling the luscious melons that popped out. The salesman followed suit energetically.

Next Berg circled her navel with his tongue. The salesman licked her whole stomach, trying not to drool.

Next Berg pulled up her teeny-weeny skirt, feeling the soft down of her inner thighs. The salesman followed, the slight tang of her pussy almost driving him insane.

Next Berg pulled out his pecker and folded it in half. The salesman sighed. "What color car d'you want?"

•

What's the difference between "ooh" and "aah"?

About three inches.

•

A man picked up a woman in a bar, brought her back to his apartment, and led her into his bedroom. "It's your lucky night, baby," he claimed boldly. "I'm going to fuck your brains out."

A half an hour later she pulled a feather out of the pillow and began tapping him on the forehead with it.

"What on earth are you doing?" he asked.

"To use your terms," she explained, "I'm beating *your* brains out."

•

A young man had always been plagued with insecurities about the size of his endowment. Deciding to take matters into his own hands, he went to a doctor and announced his desire to have his penis surgically enlarged.

The doctor checked things out and informed the patient that the only real surgical possibility was to implant a section of baby-elephant trunk.

Rather radical, agreed the young man, but he was

adamant in his desire to proceed with the operation whatever the risk.

The surgery went off without a hitch, and after a month of recuperation, the man decided it was time to try out his new equipment in the field.

He asked a lovely young woman of his acquaintance out to dinner at an elegant restaurant. They were enjoying appetizers and quiet conversation when his new organ, which had been comfortably resting in his left pants leg, whipped out over the table, grabbed a hard roll, and just as speedily disappeared from sight.

"Wow!" exclaimed his date, clearly impressed. "Can you do that again?"

"Sure," answered the fellow, trying to sound nonchalant, "but I don't know if my asshole can stand another hard roll."

•

The businessman spent a good half an hour in the hotel lounge bragging to the hooker about how big his dick was. Finally she suggested they retire to his room and check it out, and he willingly agreed.

The guy stripped off his clothes, jumped on top of the hooker, entered her, and said triumphantly, "Why don't you open your mouth, baby, so I can see the end of my prick?"

"Open my mouth?" scoffed the hooker. "Why don't you wiggle your ass so I can *feel* it?"

•

Graffiti: "I'm ten inches long and three inches wide. Interested?"

Reply: "Fascinated. How big is your dick?"

•

What do a cobra and a two-inch dick have in common?

No one wants to fuck with either of them.

•

Three construction workers, two black and one white, went across the street during their lunch break to buy a lottery ticket. They couldn't decide which numbers to play until Jermaine proposed they use the length of their dicks. "Put down seven for me," he said.

"Okay," said Kendrick. "That's ten for me."

"Make mine a three," said Chuck, the white guy. So they bet on seven-ten-three—and it won ten thousand bucks.

Of course they had to have a few drinks to celebrate after work. "You are lucky sons of bitches that I have a nice seven-incher," crowed Jermaine over a beer.

"You wouldn't be anywhere without my big boy," Kendrick reminded them with a sly smile.

"Talk about luck!" said Chuck happily. "What if I hadn't had a hard-on!?!"

•

Why shouldn't you go down on a twelve-inch cock?

You might get foot-in-mouth disease.

•

Once there was a woman who couldn't get enough, so she put an ad in the paper. The next afternoon a man came to her front door, and she asked him to pull down his pants. "I'm sorry, buddy," she explained as she showed him out, "but it has to be six feet long. Come back in a week."

A week passed and the doorbell rang again. "Hmmm . . . two feet. Come back in a week and we'll see what we can do," murmured the woman.

Another week went by, and when the doorbell rang she found the man with his dick wrapped around his neck. "Not bad," conceded the woman, "but you've still got a foot to go."

"Hold on a sec," asked the man. "I brought a crank with me." Inserting his penis, he finally stretched it out to a full six feet.

"Okay, fella," she said with a smile. "Come on back to my room."

So she undressed and the man got an erection and strangled himself.

•

A guy found a tarnished brass lamp lying on the beach one day. Being the ever-hopeful type, he rubbed it a few times, and to his delight a genie materialized. "Your command, my Lord?" prompted the spirit, bowing low. "You may have your heart's desire."

Without a second's hesitation, the man put in his request. "I want a penis that touches the ground."

So the genie cut his legs off.

•

What do you call a man with a six-inch tongue who can breathe through his ears?

Sweetheart.

•

Henry was delighted to encounter a young woman who accepted his proposal of marriage, since he was sensitive about his wooden leg and had been a bit afraid that no one would have him. In fact he couldn't quite bring himself to tell his fiancée about his leg when he slipped the engagement ring on her finger, nor when she bought the wedding dress, nor when they selected the time and place. All he kept saying was, "Darling, I've got a big surprise for you," at which she would blush and smile bewitchingly.

The wedding day finally arrived, and eventually the newlyweds found themselves alone in their hotel room. "Now don't forget, Henry, you promised me a big surprise," giggled the bride, slipping between the sheets.

Speechless now that the moment had arrived, Henry turned out the lights, unstrapped his artificial leg, got into bed, and placed his wife's hand on the stump.

"Hmmmm," she murmured, "that *is* a surprise. But pass me the Vaseline jar and I'll see what I can do."

RUDE AND CRUDE WHITE MALES

What's a redneck's idea of a seven-course meal?
A hot dog and a six-pack.

•

A pretty woman moved into town. She was so resistant to any advances by the local menfolk that they decided there must be something wrong with her sexual apparatus, maybe that she was a hermaphrodite. One guy finally talked her into to going out to a movie with him, and was delighted when on the drive back she explained she urgently had to go to the bathroom. As she squatted in the bushes beside the car, he figured this was his chance to check out her anatomy and snuck around the rear. Sure enough there was a long thing hanging down between her legs, and he reached out and grabbed it. "So!" he exclaimed weakly.

"You didn't tell me you were a peeping Tom," she said tartly.

"And you didn't tell me you had to take a shit."

•

Why did the coed nickname her boyfriend "Miller Lite?"

Tasted good, but wasn't very filling.

•

A man walked into a bar and started up a conversation with an attractive woman. Pretty soon he confided that he was recently divorced. "My wife and I just weren't sexually compatible," he explained. "I wanted to experiment, you know, try new things, but my wife just wasn't into it. Nice girl, but totally traditional."

The woman's eyes widened as she listened to this tale of marital incompatibility. "That's pretty amazing," she said. "I got divorced a year ago myself, for the same reason. My husband was a total stick-in-the-mud when it came to experimenting sexually." Dropping her voice to a whisper, she confessed to her new acquaintance, "He didn't even like me to be on top."

"Wow, this is *great*!" exclaimed the guy. "You and I are really on the same wavelength. What do you say we go back to my place and get it on?"

"Fine by me," she agreed.

Back at his apartment he issued very specific instructions. "Here's what I want you to do. Take off all your clothes, climb up on my bed, get on your hands and knees, and count to ten."

She obeyed exactly. "Ten," she called out, tingling with excitement. Nothing happened. "Yoo hoo . . . ten," she called sweetly. Then, "I'm waiting. . . ."

"Jeez, I'm sorry," blurted her new acquaintance. "I got off already. I just shat in your purse."

•

Little Julie was the apple of her father's eye, especially since she had been born with a heart condition and had always required pampering and special care. When she announced her engagement, Julie's father took it kind of hard, and on the wedding day he took the groom aside for a little talk.

"Listen, I don't know if Julie's told you this," he revealed, "but my little girl's awfully delicate. I think you ought to know that she has acute angina."

"Boy, that's good," said the groom with a grin, "because she sure doesn't have any tits!"

•

Terribly agitated, Jack rushed into his dentist's examining room and ushered the hygienist firmly to the door. Once he was alone with the doctor, he unzipped his fly and gingerly pulled out his dick.

"Jack, Jack," said the dentist, taken aback. "I'm a dentist. If you think you have V.D., you need to see your regular doctor."

"It's not V.D.," gasped Jack, "and you've gotta help me. There's a tooth stuck in it."

•

Laura sized up the guy coming over to her at the singles bar as a real sleazeball, and sure enough he sidled up to her with a leer and said, "Hey baby, I'd really like to get into your pants tonight."

"I don't think so, buddy," she replied. "One asshole in there's enough."

•

Did you hear about the masochist who said to her boyfriend, "Give me nine inches and make it hurt."

So he screwed her twice and slapped her.

•

A man in a crowded elevator accidentally jabbed the woman next to him in the chest with his elbow. He rather liked what he felt, though, so he leaned over and whispered, "If the rest of you's as firm as your tits, I'd love to fuck you."

Without missing a beat, she snapped, "If your dick's as hard as your elbow, I'll give you my phone number."

•

What's a rude white boy's idea of foreplay?

Pulling off a woman's panty hose.

•

Once the Bionic Woman had to take an overnight train trip. She entered her compartment without noticing that the berth above her was occupied by a young man. Peering through the curtains, he was quite chagrined to see her remove her wig, false eyelashes, glass eye, padded brassiere, mechanical hand, and bionic leg. When she got into bed and pulled up the covers, she caught sight of the peeping Tom and cried out in alarm, "Oh my goodness! What do you want?"

"You know damn well what I want," he snarled. "Unscrew it and toss it up here."

•

What's a man's definition of eternity?

The length of time between when *he* comes and *she* leaves.

WHITE MALES WHO ARE INFERIOR TO WOMEN

Why do men have dicks?
So women will talk to them.

•

What should you give a man who has everything?
A woman to show him how to work it.

•

A woman went to the gynecologist and was told she was in perfect health and had the body of an eighteen-year-old. She was so excited she ran home to tell her husband.

"What about your fat ass?" he asked.

"Oh, he didn't say anything about you," she replied.

•

Why do black widow spiders kill their males after mating?

To stop the snoring before it starts.

•

The newlyweds were undressing in their honeymoon suite on the wedding night. The new husband, who was a big bruiser of a guy, tossed his pants over to his wife and said, "Here, put these on."

Puzzled, she pulled them on and said, "These would fit two of me—I can't wear these pants."

"That's right," said the husband, "and don't you forget it. I'm the one who wears the pants in this family."

With that the wife threw her pants over to his side of the bed and said, "Try these on."

Finding he could only get them up as far as his knees, her husband said, "Hell, I can't even get *into* your pants.

"That's right," she snapped, "and that's the way it's going to be until your goddamn attitude changes."

•

Ever realized that Ginger Rogers did everything Fred Astaire did . . . only backward and in high heels?

•

What are the three best things about being a woman?

You can bleed without cutting yourself;
You can bury a bone without digging a hole;
And you can make a man come without calling him.

•

Why is marriage like divorce?

They both begin when a man finds a woman who really understands him.

•

A little girl walked into the bathroom, saw her father in the shower, and ran to her mother screaming, "Mommy, Mommy! Daddy has a big ugly worm hanging out of his wee-wee!"

"That isn't a worm, sweetheart," said her mother reassuringly. "That's part of your daddy's body and a very important part. If your daddy didn't have one of those, you wouldn't be here." Stopping to reflect for a moment, she added, "and come to think of it . . . neither would I."

•

A woman of 30 thinks of having children. What's a man the same age thinking of?

Dating children.

•

A young couple hadn't been married for long when, one morning, the man came up behind his wife as she got out of the shower and grabbed her by the buttocks. "Y'know, honey," he said smugly, "if you firmed these up a little bit, you wouldn't have to keep using your girdle."

Her feelings were so hurt that she refused to speak to him for the rest of the day.

Only a week later he again stepped into the bathroom just as she was drying off from her shower. Grabbing both breasts, he said, "Y'know, honey, if you firmed these up a bit, you wouldn't have to keep wearing a bra."

The young wife was infuriated, but had to wait till the next morning to exact her revenge. Waiting till her husband stepped out of the shower, she grabbed him by the dick and hissed, "Y'know, honey, if you firmed this up a little bit, I wouldn't have to keep using your brother."

•

Why do bachelors like smart women?

Opposites attract.

•

"Sheila," asked Lucy thoughtfully one day, "what would you do if you caught another woman in bed with your husband?"

"With Ralph?" Sheila thought it over. "Let's see: I'd break her cane, shoot her seeing eye dog, and call a cab to take her back to the institution she escaped from."

•

Why is it lucky there are female astronauts?

So someone will ask directions if the ship gets lost in space.

•

Sam and Cindy grew up next door to each other and as they grew older each constantly tried to one-up the other. If Sam got a jungle gym, Cindy got a swing set, and so on, until the contest became a very expensive one for both sets of parents. Finally Sam's father asked what was going on, and when Sam explained it, a big grin came over his face.

Next Saturday Cindy whizzed down the sidewalk on a brand new tricycle. "Nyaah, nyaah," she taunted, "look what I've got."

"So?" retorted Sam. "I've got something you'll never have—look!" And he pulled down his pants and showed her.

Realizing she'd been outdone, Cindy ran into her house sobbing. Her father picked her up and tried to comfort her. Getting the whole story out of her, he smiled and whispered something in her ear.

The next day Sam spotted Cindy in the backyard and decided to rub it in. "I've got one of these and you don't," he teased, pulling his pants down again.

"Big deal," said Cindy haughtily, pulling her skirt up

and her underpants down. "My Daddy says that with one of *these* I can have as many of *those* as I want."

•

Why do women have such big tits and tight pussies?

Because men have such big mouths and little peckers.

•

What's been the most effective means of birth control since the days of Adam and Eve?

Laughter.

•

Who enjoys sex more, the man or the woman?

The woman.

How can I prove it? When your ear itches and you put your little finger in and wiggle it around and take it out again, what feels better, your finger or your ear?

•

A certain couple loved to compete with other, comparing their achievements in every aspect of their lives: salaries, athletic abilities, social accomplishments, and so on. Everything was a contest, and the husband sank into a deep depression because he had yet to win a single one. Finally he sought professional counsel, explaining to the shrink that while he wouldn't mind losing once in a while, his unbroken string of defeats had him pretty down.

"Simple enough. All we have to do is devise a game that you can't possibly lose." The shrink thought for a moment, then proposed a pissing contest. "Whoever can pee higher on the wall wins—and how could any woman win?"

Running home, the husband called up, "Darling, I've got a new game!"

"Oooh, I love games," she squealed, running down the stairs. "What is it?"

"C'mon out here," he instructed, pulling her around to the patio. "We're going to stand here, piss on this wall, and whoever makes the highest mark wins."

"What fun! I'll go first." The woman proceeded to lift her dress, then her leg, and pee on the wall about six inches up from the ground. She turned to him expectantly.

"Okay, now it's my turn," said the beleaguered husband eagerly. He unzipped his fly, pulled out his penis, and was just about to pee when his wife interrupted.

"Hang on a sec," she called out merrily. "No hands allowed!"

•

Why did God make man first?

Because he didn't want a woman looking over his shoulder and making him improve on the job.

•

Shatzkin was used to the occasional late-night call, usually from a client who'd had an accident of some sort, but this night it was an agitated woman obviously in the middle of a violent argument with her husband.

"Tell me, Mr. Shatzkin," she yelled over the noise of her mate's ranting in the background, "if a husband leaves his wife, is she or is she not legally entitled to the house and its contents?"

"I can't give such advice over the phone, especially without knowing the particulars of the case," the lawyer pointed out reasonably. "Call my office in the morning and we'll set up an appointment."

The background roars had subsided, and the woman continued without skipping a beat. "She's also entitled to the time-share, both cars, and the joint savings account? Thank you very much." And she hung up with a triumphant smile.

•

The real-estate mogul was delighted by the comely new receptionist, and proceeded to turn all of his charms upon her. Within a few weeks, however, he grew extremely displeased at her growing tardiness. "Listen, baby," he roared one morning, "we may have gone to bed together a few times, but who said you could start coming in late?"

The secretary replied sweetly, "My lawyer."

•

Why is rape so rare?

Because a woman can run faster with her dress up than a man with his pants down.

•

Why's beauty more important than brains for a woman?

Because plenty of men are stupid, but not very many are blind.

•

Why is swapping partners with your girlfriends not such a good idea?

It's *sooooo* depressing when you get your man back.

•

The horny college kid borrowed his roommate's car, scraped together every penny he could find, and picked up his date at her parents' house. He took her to the nicest place in town, but grew more and more upset when she proceeded to order everything pricey on the menu: fancy mixed drinks, lobster, champagne, the works. Finally he blurted, "Does your mother feed you like this at home?"

"Nope," she replied with a demure smile, "but my Mom's not trying to get laid either."

•

Timmy spent nearly ten years wooing Rosa, the girl of his dreams. Finally, after she'd had plenty of time to fool around, she agreed to marry him. After the wedding they got into bed, snuggled up, and the bridegroom was thrilled when Rosa asked sweetly, "Timmy, now that we're married, can I do anything I like?"

"Of course, sweetheart," he replied with a tender smile.

So she rolled over and went to sleep.

•

Why did God give women nipples?

To make suckers out of men.

•

A young country girl came to town for a day. She was window shopping when a beautiful pair of red shoes caught her eye, and as she stood admiring them the clerk came out and asked if he could help her. The girl admitted that she'd spent all her money but that she'd do anything to get her hands on those red shoes.

The clerk thought it over for a moment. "I think we can work out a deal," he told her. "Go lie down on the couch in the back room." Soon he came in and closed the door. "So do you want those shoes bad enough to put out for them?" he asked. When she nodded he pulled down his pants, exposing a hard-on about nine inches long. "Honey, I'll screw with this big cock of mine until you squirm with pleasure and scream in ecstasy and go wild with desire."

"I don't get much of a kick out of sex, but go right ahead," said the girl, spreading her legs and lying back. Sure she couldn't last long, the salesman started pumping away, but she lay there like a dishrag. Pretty soon he'd come twice and began to worry about getting soft, so he started going at it for all he was worth. Sure enough he felt her arms go around his neck and her legs tighten around his waist. "Best fuck you've ever had, right?" chortled the guy. "In a couple of seconds you'll be coming like crazy."

"Oh, no, it's not that," said the girl. "I'm just trying on my new shoes."

•

What are three things a woman can do that a man can't?

1) Have a baby.
2) Have her period.
3) Get laid when she's dead.

WHITE MALES WHO ARE SUPERIOR TO WOMEN

How can you tell women have less brains than men?
Because they don't have a dick to put them in.

•

What could Mark Fuhrman do that a black woman couldn't?
Get O. J. off.

•

Why do men think the contraceptive sponge is so swell?
Because after sex the woman can get up and wash the dishes.

•

Why are women so bad in math?

Because all their life they've been told that this [hold your hands a few inches apart] is eight inches.

•

One night this guy got so bombed that he went from the bar to the local tattoo parlor. And there the tattoo artist followed his instructions to have "I Love You" tattooed on his dick.

The next night he and his wife were making love when she suddenly went wild with rage. "What's the matter, honey," he asked tenderly.

"I cook for you, I clean for you, I do everything for you," she screamed, "and now you're trying to put words in my mouth!"

•

Heard anything about the "morning-after" pill for men?

It works by changing your blood type.

•

Adam and Eve were strolling in the Garden of Eden after dinner one evening when Eve turned anxiously to her mate. "Adam," she asked, "tell me the truth. Do you love me?"

Adam shrugged. "Who else?"

•

What's a man's idea of housework?

Lifting his legs so a woman can vacuum underneath them.

•

Mike was touching up the paint in the bathroom one weekend when the brush slipped out of his hand, leaving a stripe across the toilet seat. So Mike painted the whole seat over, and went off to a ball game.

His wife happened to get home early, went upstairs to pee, and found herself firmly stuck to the toilet seat. At six o'clock Mike found her there, furious and embarrassed, but was unable to dislodge her for fear of tearing the skin.

With considerable difficulty Mike managed to get her into the back seat of the car and then into a wheelchair at the hospital, where she was wheeled into a room and maneuvered, on her knees, onto an examining table. At this point the resident entered and surveyed the scene.

"What do you think, Doc?" broke in the nervous husband.

"Nice, very nice," he commented, stroking his chin. "But why the cheap frame?"

•

Why does a woman rub her eyes when she wakes up in the morning?

Because she doesn't have balls to scratch.

•

Chip was cruising down the street in a brand new Corvette when a friend spotted him and waved him over. "Nice wheels," he said admiringly. "Where'd you get 'em?"

"See, I was hitchhiking up to Encino when this beautiful girl pulled over and picked me up," explained the lucky guy. "We drove for a while and then she pulled off onto a country road, and got out of the car, and asked me to kiss her. I couldn't believe it."

"So did you kiss her?" pressed his friend.

"Sure I did," Chip went on, "and get a load of what happened next. She stripped down to her panties and told me I could have anything she had."

"So?"

"Well I knew the panties wouldn't fit me, so I took the car."

•

What's a man's definition of a wife?

An attachment you screw on the bed to get the housework done.

•

What do men think is the best thing about Women's Liberation?

It gives you girls something to do in your spare time.

•

How many men does it take to mop a floor?

None. It's a woman's job.

•

Why are men starting to endorse female candidates?
They figure they won't have to pay such big salaries!

•

Eager to make her mark in the world of business, the attractive new MBA took a job as executive assistant to the middle-aged owner of a fast-growing computer software company. She found the work challenging and the travel interesting, but was extremely annoyed by her boss's tendency to treat her in public as though she were his girlfriend rather than a professional associate.

This was especially irritating in restaurants, where he would insist on ordering for her, and on calling her Dearest or Darling within earshot of the waiters. When she told him how much it bothered her, he promised to stop, but the patronizing behavior continued. Finally, as he led her into a four-star restaurant, she took matters into her own hands.

"Where would you like to sit, sweetheart?" he asked, with a wink at the maître d'.

"Gee," she replied, "anywhere you say, Dad."

•

What's the definition of a faithful husband?
One whose alimony checks never bounce.

HOPELESSLY NAIVE WHITE MALES

In Dallas on business, Jerry picked up a lovely girl in the hotel bar and took her up to his room. After a few drinks, the girl sat on his lap. "Would you like to hug me?" she asked.

"Of course," panted Jerry, pulling her close.

"And would you like to kiss me?"

"You bet," said Jerry, planting a long kiss on her lips.

"Okay, honey," she continued, "brace yourself, because here comes the fifty-dollar question."

•

One night little Johnny walked in on his parents while they were screwing. "Daddy," he cried, "what are you and Mommy doing?"

"Uh . . . we're making a little sister for you to play with," stammered his father.

"Oh, neat," said Johnny, and went back to bed.

The next day his dad came home to find the little boy sobbing his eyes out on the front porch. "What's wrong, Johnny?" he asked, picking him up.

"You know the little sister you and Mommy made me?"

"Yes," said his father, blushing.

The little boy wailed, "Today the milkman ate it."

•

Rick was trying real hard to get the best-looking cheerleader in school to go out on a date with him. She finally agreed, but only on condition that he arrange a date for her best friend too. That was fine with Rick, but when Friday night came around he hadn't been able to line anyone up so he asked his retarded brother Bill if he would help him out. "Why sure," said Bill, "but you know, I've never been out with a girl before."

"No problem," said Rick. "Just do everything I do."

Off the four of them go to the drive-in, and when Rick started kissing his date, Bill followed suit. Soon Rick had the cheerleader's bra undone, so Bill undid his date's. Next, Rick was feeling inside her panties, but when Bill tried to follow suit, his date told him to quit.

"Why?" asked Bill, anxiously noting that his brother was getting quite a head start in the front seat.

"I have my period," she said.

"You're what?"

"I'm bleeding down there," she explained, blushing.

"This I gotta see," said Bill. He turned on the headlights, dragged his date out in front of the car, and pulled down her pants. White-faced, he said, "Hell, I'd be bleeding, too, if my dick were chopped off!"

•

"Linda, you've got some explaining to do," said the husband when he got home from work. "I saw you at a restaurant with a strange man today. Now I want an explanation, and I want the truth."

"Make up your mind," she said calmly. "Which one do you want?"

•

A young couple was parked on Lovers Lane. The young man turned admiringly to his pretty date and said, "Gee, you smell good. You wearing perfume or something?"

The girl blushed charmingly and confessed that she was wearing a new perfume that she'd bought especially with him in mind. "You smell good, too," she said. "What do you have on?"

"Well, I have a hard-on," he blurted, "but I didn't know you could smell it."

•

"Nice threads, man," commented Malcolm when his buddy showed up one day in a snappy new suit. "Where'd you pick 'em up?"

Calvin beamed. "My old lady got them for me. Pretty sharp, huh?"

"I'll say. What was the occasion?"

"Got me," admitted Calvin with a cheerful shrug. "I came home from work early the other day and there they were, hanging over the chair in the bedroom."

•

When sixteen-year-old Gary came home with the news that he'd gotten laid for the first time, his mother was less than pleased. Slapping him across the face, she sent him off to his room without any supper. When Gary's father got home and heard the news, he went up to see his son.

"Well, Gary," he admonished, secretly pleased, "I hope you learned something from this experience."

"You bet I did," admitted his son. "Next time I'll use Vaseline. My ass is killing me!"

•

"Father," whispered the young man on the eve of his wedding, "what am I supposed to do? I'm a little nervous."

"Don't worry about a thing," consoled the understanding Dad. "All you have to do is take that thing you used to play with when you were a little boy and stick it where your wife urinates."

"Wow, that sounds easy enough. Thanks, Dad," the boy said confidently. So he hung up the phone and threw his G.I. Joe doll in the toilet.

•

This guy came into work one day with a fistful of cigars and started passing them out left and right to celebrate the birth of his son. "Congratulations, Eric," said his boss. "How much did the baby weigh?"

"Four and a half pounds," reported the father proudly.

"Gee, that's kind of small."

"Hey, what'd you expect?" retorted Eric indignantly. "We've only been married three months."

•

Definition of henpecked:
A sterile husband afraid to tell his pregnant wife.

•

"Do you smoke after sex?" asked the girl of the man she'd just met in a bar.

"Got me," he admitted. "I never looked."

•

The innocent hick finally decided to make the long trip into town and find himself a nice girl to settle down with. Without too much trouble he found a willing woman at the corner bar and off they went to the Justice of the Peace. He rented a room in a hotel on Main Street, they screwed all night long, and the farm boy went to sleep a happy man.

But the next morning his new bride woke up to the sound of her husband sitting bolt upright in bed and sobbing his heart out. "What's wrong, honey?" she asked.

"One night," he moaned, "and it's all used up."

•

What was the first thing Adam said to Eve?
"Stand back—I don't know how big this thing's gonna get!"

•

So what was the first thing Eve said to Adam?
"You could get by with a smaller fig leaf."

•

What's a naive guy's idea of a hand job?
A girl who sucks on his fingers.

•

A certain couple wanted a baby more than anything in the world, but all their efforts came to nothing. One day they were out for a stroll when they spotted another couple pushing their beautiful new baby in a stroller. Going over and admitting their heart's desire, they shyly asked the other couple if they had any advice.

"There are a few tricks to it," conceded the new father. "For one thing, you gotta be eight inches long."

"No problem," said the aspiring parent.

"Secondly," the other guy went on, "you gotta be at least three-and-a-half inches around."

"So *that's* the problem," exclaimed the fellow, turning to his wife. "We've been letting too much light in!"

•

Mr. Smith came home early one day, only to find his new bride firmly grasping the penises of two of his friends with each hand, receiving a third man from the rear, and going down on a fourth man who lay moaning beneath her.

"Oh, darling, how could you?" asked her husband reprovingly.

"You know, dear," she answered, looking up briefly, "I've always been something of a flirt."

•

When did the white guy suspect he might be marrying the wrong girl?

When she showed up at the church with male bridesmaids.

•

What was another clue that night?

When his bride told him they were seeing too much of each other.

•

At her annual checkup, the attractive woman was told by the new doctor that it was necessary to take a rectal temperature. The patient agreed, but a few minutes later protested, "Doctor, that's not my rectum!"

"And it's not my thermometer," admitted the doctor with a grin.

At that moment the patient's husband, who had

come to pick her up, came into the examining room. "What the hell's going on in here?" he demanded, taking stock of the situation.

"Just taking your wife's temperature," explained the doctor coolly.

"Okay, doctor," said the man grudgingly, "but that thing better have numbers on it."

•

This fellow had been assured by his fiancée that she was a virgin, but given the state of modern morals, he didn't completely trust her. So he devised a little quiz for their wedding night. Pulling down his pajamas, he asked, "Honey, can you tell me what this is?"

"A wee-wee," she answered coyly.

Delighted by her naïveté, the new husband corrected her gently. "No, sweetheart. It's a penis."

"Huh-uh, it's a wee-wee," insisted his bride, shaking her head.

Slightly annoyed, he shook his head. "It's time for you to learn a few things, dearest. Now this is a penis."

"No way," she retorted. "It's not half as big as some of the penises I've seen."

•

A young man was brought up by his father in the Australian outback. Not wanting the boy to get into trouble, the father told him to stay away from women. "They have teeth down there," he explained, and let the impressionable young boy's imagination do the rest.

Eventually, however, the old man died, and seeing his acquaintances getting married and starting families, the young man decided it was time to get on with it. So he rode into the nearest town and found himself a willing girl—who was rather disappointed when the consummation of their wedding night consisted of a peck on the cheek. The second night she dolled herself up in a sheer negligee, only to have her new husband again kiss her on the cheek, roll over, and fall fast asleep. On the third night she caught him before the snores began and proceeded to give him a brief lecture on the birds and the bees and his conjugal duties.

"Oh, no you don't!" he cried, sitting up in alarm and pulling the bedclothes tightly around himself. "I know about you women! You've got teeth down there, and I'm not coming anywhere near."

Being a good-humored sort, his bride roared with laughter, then invited her husband to come around and see for himself. Warily he circled the bed and proceeded to check out her anatomy with great care. Finally he stuck his head up.

"You're right," he proclaimed. "You've got no teeth, and your gums are in terrible condition!"

•

As the newlywed couple was checking into the hotel for their honeymoon, another couple at the desk offered to show them around the town that night. Thanking them for the kind offer, the bridegroom explained that it was their wedding night and that they'd prefer to take a rain check.

When the second couple came down to breakfast the next morning they were astonished to catch sight of the groom in the hotel bar apparently drowning his sorrows. "Why, you should be the happiest man in the world today," they said, coming over to him.

"Yesterday I was," said the man mournfully, "but this morning, without realizing it, I put three ten-dollar bills on the pillow and got up to get dressed."

"Hey, cheer up, she probably didn't even notice."

"That's the problem," the groom went on. "Without even thinking, she gave me five dollars change."

•

Three fathers-to-be met at the water cooler and got to talking. "I was on top the night we conceived," confided one of the men, "and our obstetrician says we're going to have a girl."

"Is that so?" commented the second guy. "Louise was on top that night, and her doctor assured us it's going to be a boy."

"Oh, shit," moaned the third man. "Just my luck—we're gonna have puppies!"

•

Not long after his creation, Adam was taking a stroll around the Garden of Eden, and he noticed two birds billing and cooing up in a tree. Adam called up, "Hey, what're those two birds doing, Lord?"

"They're making love, Adam," God told him.

A little later Adam wandered into a meadow, where he saw a bull and a cow going at it hot and heavy. "Lord, what are those animals up to?" he called.

"They're making love, Adam," God told him.

Adam thought for a minute, and then asked, "It looks kind of fun. How come I don't have anyone to make love with?"

"You've got a point," conceded God, "and we'll do something about it. When you wake up tomorrow, things will be different."

Sure enough, when Adam woke up the next morning he found Eve asleep next to him. "Hey there," he said, "come with me." And he grabbed her hand and dragged her off into the bushes.

A few minutes later Adam emerged from the shrubbery, looking very depressed. "Lord," he called up, "what's a headache?"

•

Ned came home early one day and found his wife in bed naked, sweating, and visibly distressed. "Bobbie, what's wrong?" he asked, pale with alarm.

"Uh . . . I think I'm having a heart attack," she stammered.

"Hang in there, honey, I'll call the doctor," he assured her, and ran downstairs to get the number.

He was just dialing when his ten-year-old burst into the room and yelled, "Daddy, Daddy, there's a naked man in the closet." Going back upstairs, Ned opened the closet door. There, sure enough, stood his friend, naked as a jaybird.

"For God's sake, Alan," scolded Ned. "My wife's in there having a heart attack and here you are sneaking around scaring the kids."

ABSURDLY SELF-ABSORBED WHITE MALES

How can you tell soap operas are fictional?

In real life, men aren't affectionate out of bed.

•

Why is sleeping with a man like a soap opera?

Just when it's getting interesting, they're finished until next time.

•

Harvey's topics of conversation had always been limited to work and sports, and once he retired he spent every waking minute attending events, glued to the sports channel, or reading *Sports Illustrated*. At first Shirley was glad he had a hobby to keep him busy, but his obsession grew irritating, and eventually infuriating.

One night as they lay in bed together, Harvey raptly watching a Romanian soccer match, Shirley decided she'd had enough. She got up, walked across the room, and unplugged the television.

"Hey, what do you think you're doing?" he protested.

"Listen to me, Harvey," she demanded. "I'm sick of sports. You've barely talked to me in weeks, not to mention actually touching me. It's time to talk about sex."

"Uh, okay," agreed her startled mate. "So how often do you think Michael Jordan gets laid?"

•

Why do men like love at first sight?

It saves them a lot of time.

•

With one look at his voluptuous new patient, all the gynecologist's professional ethics went right out the window. Instructing her to undress completely, he began to stroke the soft skin of her inner thigh. "Do you know what I'm doing?" he asked softly.

"Checking for any dermatological abnormalities, right?"

"Right," crooned the doctor, beginning to fondle her breasts and gently pinch her nipples. "And now?"

"Looking for any lumps that might be cancerous."

"Right you are," reassured the doctor, placing her feet in the stirrups, pulling out his cock, and entering her. "And do you know what I'm doing now?"

"Yup," she said, looking down. "Catching herpes."

•

Why do so many men never marry?

They just can't find women who love them as much as they do.

•

The newlyweds undressed and got into bed. "Sweetheart," asked the new wife, "could you please hand me that jar of Vaseline over there?"

"Baby, you aren't going to need any Vaseline," he growled amorously. But at her insistence he handed it over, and she proceeded to smear it liberally all over her crotch.

After watching this procedure, the husband asked the wife a favor. "Remember that long string of pearls I gave you for an engagement present? Could you get them out of the bureau drawer for me?"

"Of course, lover," replied his bride, "but whatever do you want them for?"

"Well," he explained, looking down at the Vaseline smeared all over her, "if you think I'm going into a mess like that without chains, you're crazy!"

•

What's the definition of conceit?

A mosquito with a hard-on floating down the river on his back and yelling, "Open the drawbridge!"

•

What's even more conceited?

The mosquito's brother, who sexually attacks a lioness and then whispers in her ear, "Did I hurt you, babe?"

•

The handsome actor had no qualms about pointing out that he was a perfect physical specimen. "In fact, I'm so perfect I had my whole self insured. Why, my dick alone is insured with Lloyds of London for $50,000."

"Smart," commented a lady friend who was thoroughly fed up with his boasting. "What did you do with the money?"

•

What's the definition of a macho guy?

Someone who's been circumcised with pinking shears.

•

What's another symptom?

When he insists on jogging home afterward.

•

One day a certain housewife became extremely horny while going about the routine business of cleaning the house. Unfortunately her husband was still at work, so she resorted to stripping off all her clothes and masturbating furiously in the middle of the living room floor. She got pretty worked up, and was writhing and moaning when her husband walked in.

"Honey," he asked, looking up from the day's mail, "when you've finished vacuuming, could you get started on dinner?"

•

Why is a clitoris like Antarctica?

Most men know it's down there, but not many really care.

•

After going through Lamaze, LeBoyer, and LaLeche classes with his expectant wife, the proud new father remained by his wife's bedside throughout the labor and birth, bonding with the newborn child. Wanting to be as sympathetic and sensitive as possible, he took his wife's hand and said emotionally, "Tell me, darling, how was it? How did it actually feel to give birth?"

"Smile," his wife instructed. "Smile as hard as you can."

Beaming beatifically at his wife and newborn son, the father commented, "That's not so hard."

She continued, "Now stick your fingers in the corners of your mouth." He obeyed,

"Now stretch your lips as wide as they'll go," his wife ordered.

"Still not too tough," he said.

"Now pull them over your head."

•

Men: Give 'em an inch . . . and they add it to their own.

•

How did the WASP economize on his honeymoon?
He went alone.

COMPLETELY MISCELLANEOUS WHITE MALES

A woman went into the neighborhood grocery store and asked the grocer for a can of cat food. Knowing that she didn't have a cat, the grocer asked why she was buying the stuff. "It's for my husband's lunch," was the answer.

Shocked, the grocer said, "You can't feed cat food to your husband. It'll kill him!"

"I've been giving it to Sheldon for a week now and he likes it fine," was her answer, and each day the woman continued to come in and purchase a can of cat food for her husband's lunch.

It wasn't too much later that the grocer happened to be scanning the obituary column in the local paper and noticed that the woman's husband had passed away. When the woman came into the store he couldn't resist saying, "I'm sorry to hear about your husband, but I warned you that he'd die if you kept feeding him cat food."

"It wasn't the cat food that killed him," she retorted. "He broke his neck trying to lick his ass!"

•

A Texan comes into a bar in the Northeast and it only takes him a few drinks to start boasting about the superior size of just about everything in Texas. "Did you know our women have tits forty feet across?" he asks proudly.

"Oh, really," says the woman next to him politely.

"Well, they only miss it by this much," allows the Texan, holding his fingers about two inches apart. "And our women have cunts so big they can hold a dick twenty feet long."

"No kidding," she responds dryly.

"Well not quite, but they only miss it by about this much," says the Texan, indicating another two inches.

"Say, I bet you didn't know that the women in these parts have babies out their assholes," offers the local.

"Is that so?" says the Texan, astonished.

"Well not really," she admits good-naturedly, "but they only miss it by about this much. . . ."

•

What goes "Ha! Ha! Thump! Thump!"?

A man laughing his balls off.

•

How do you force a man to do push-ups?

Put the remote control between his legs.

•

Leonard desperately wanted to become a doctor and had really crammed for his medical boards, so he wasn't in the least fazed by the question: "Name the three advantages of breast milk."

Quickly he wrote: 1) It contains the optimum balance of nutrients for the newborn child. He added, 2) Since it is contained within the mother's body, it is protected from germs and helps develop the child's immune system. Then Leonard was stumped. Sitting back and racking his brains until he'd broken a sweat, he finally scribbled, 3) It comes in such nice containers.

•

What do electric train sets and women's breasts have in common?

Both were intended for children, but it's the fathers who play with them.

•

When is it justified for a woman to spit in a man's face?

When his mustache is on fire.

•

The salesgirl at the Pink Pussycat boutique didn't bat an eye when the customer purchased an artificial vagina. "What're you going to use it for?" she asked.

"None of your business," answered the customer, thoroughly offended.

"Calm down, buddy," soothed the salesgirl. "The only reason I'm asking is that if it's food, we don't have to charge you sales tax."

•

Did you hear about the guy who was given three weeks to live?

He picked the first two weeks of August and the last week of December.

•

Why is a woman's blind date like a snowstorm?

She never knows how many inches she'll get or how long it will last.

•

What's the best defense against rape?

Beating off the attacker.

•

Carl was pacing back and forth outside the hospital delivery room door. Another nervous father finally broke the silence. "Some luck. My one week of vacation and look where I get to spend it."

"You think *you've* got bad luck?" responded Carl. "I'm on my honeymoon."

•

What should a woman give the man who has everything except brains?

Encouragement.

•

What else?

Penicillin.

•

Why are bankers such good lovers?

They've grasped that there's a substantial penalty for early withdrawal.

•

Mort knew he was probably oversensitive about the problem, but the fact was that his eyes bulged out. He went to doctor after doctor, but none seemed to know of any treatment, and in desperation he looked up "Eyes Bulging Out" in the Yellow Pages. Sure enough a doctor was listed, and a few days later Mort found himself sitting on a vinyl couch in a seedy waiting room. A little nervous about being the only patient, he reminded himself how rare the condition was and that the doctor *was* a specialist.

At long last he was admitted to the doctor's office and examined. The doctor leaned back and informed him that there was a remedy, but not an easy one. "I must cut your balls off," he said.

Mort's eyes bulged out even more as he headed for

the door. But after a few weeks of thinking it over, Mort acknowledged that his bulging eyes were what kept him from getting laid in the first place, so he decided to go ahead with the operation. So he returned for the operation, and sure enough, his eyeballs sunk back into their sockets most agreeably. In fact, he looked not only normal but actually rather handsome.

Delighted, he thanked the doctor profusely, and decided to treat his remodeled self to a new suit. "Charcoal gray pinstripe," he instructed the tailor. "Medium lapel, no cuffs,"

"Fine," said the tailor, nodding. "Come back on Tuesday."

"Aren't you going to measure me?" asked Mort.

"Nah. I've been at this over 30 years; I can tell your size just by looking," the tailor assured him.

"That's impossible," blurted Mort.

"Size forty-two jacket, right?"

"Yes," admitted Mort, amazed.

"Thirty-two-inch inseam, right?"

Mort nodded, dumbstruck.

"Thirty-six-inch waist?"

Again Mort nodded.

"And you wear size forty underwear, right?" concluded the tailor with a smile.

"Nope!" Mort told him. "Thirty-four."

"Listen, you can't fool me," said the tailor wearily. "Don't even try to put one over."

"I'm telling you, I wear size thirty-four underwear," Mort insisted.

"You *can't* wear size thirty-four underwear," protested the exasperated tailor. "Your eyes would bulge out of their sockets!"

•

After the birth of his third child, Warner decided to have a vasectomy. During the operation, one of his testicles accidentally fell on the floor, and before the nurse could scoop it back up, the doctor had stepped on it. Unfazed, the doctor simply asked the nurse for a small onion, which he proceeded to suture inside the scrotum.

Two weeks later Warner was back for his post-op checkup. "How's it going?" asked the doctor.

"I gotta tell you, I'm having some problems," admitted the patient.

"Such as?"

"Well, Doc, every time I take a leak, my eyes water; every time I come, I get heartburn; and every time I pass a Burger King, I get a hard-on!"

•

Heard about the new generic rubbers?

They're for cheap fuckers.

•

What does a man have in his pants that a woman doesn't want in her face?

Wrinkles!

•

Why does a dog lick his balls?

Because he can.

•

When Paddy O'Brian died, Father Flanagan was there to console the bereaved widow. "You know, Molly, the whole community is here to help you through this time of sorrow," he consoled her, "and of course if there's anything I can do, you know I will."

Parting her veil and drying her tearstained cheeks, the widow whispered a single request in the priest's ear. Father Flanagan blushed scarlet and refused outright, but the widow persisted and finally he gave in to her pleading. Saying, "Give me twenty-four hours," he left. And the next day he showed up at the O'Brian house with a parcel wrapped in brown paper.

The widow popped the contents into a pot on the stove, and as it was boiling away a neighbor dropped by. "I say, Molly," commented the neighbor, opening the lid, "isn't that Paddy's penis?"

"Indeed it is," confirmed Molly. "All his life I had to eat it his way, and now I'm eating it mine."

•

This 600-pound guy decides he can't go on living like a human blimp, so he seeks the advice of a clinic and goes on a drastic diet. It works; four months later he's down to 160 and feeling great. There's just one problem: He's covered with great folds of flesh where the fat used to be.

His doctor tells him not to worry. "We've got a special surgical procedure to correct the problem," the doctor reassures him. "Just come on over to the clinic."

"But Doctor," protests the onetime fatty miserably,

"I'm too embarrassed to go out in public like this. I really look weird."

"Don't give it another thought," says the doctor. "Just pull all the flesh as high as it'll go, pile it on top of your head, put on a ski hat, and come on over.

The patient follows these instructions, dying of self-consciousness, but mercifully arrives at the front desk of the clinic without provoking any comments. "The doctor will be right with you," the receptionist tells him with a friendly smile. "Say, what's that hole in the middle of your forehead?"

"My belly button," blurts the guy. "How d'ya like my tie?"

•

One day Jason burst into the house and said, "Mom! Dad! I have great news: I'm getting married to the greatest girl in the world. Florence has agreed to marry me."

But that night Jason's dad took him aside for a little chat. "I have some bad news for you son," he confessed. "See, I used to fool around a lot, and Florence's actually your half sister. I'm afraid you can't marry her."

Jason was brokenhearted, and moped around for a good six months, but eventually he started dating again. And in a year or so he came home with happy tidings. "Vickie said yes! We're getting married in October, isn't that great?"

Alas, Jason's father insisted on another private conversation and broke more bad news. "Vickie's your half sister too, son. I'm awfully sorry."

This time Jason was beside himself with anger and

grief, and he finally confessed to his mother. "At this rate I'm never going to get married," he moaned. "Every time I fall in love, Dad says the girl's my relative."

"Don't pay any attention to him, Jason. Go right ahead and marry Vickie," said his mother cheerfully. "See, I did some fooling around myself, and he's not your father."

•

What's the only thing the government can't tax?

A penis, because 95% of the time it's inactive, 5% of the time it's in the hole, and it's got two dependents and they're both nuts.

•

A young man was spending the night at the apartment of a married couple of his acquaintance. Since there was no couch, the couple offered to share their own bed with the guest, and they all retired early.

Not long afterward the wife whispered in the young man's ear, "Pull a hair from my husband's butt; if he's asleep, we can make love."

Surprised but not displeased, the young man did as instructed. Getting no response from the husband, he proceeded to make it with the wife. Not completely satisfied, the wife proposed the same course of action a second time, and later a third time, and the young guest was only too happy to oblige. His ardor was dimmed, however, when the husband rolled over and confronted the couple. "Look," he said wearily, "it's bad enough that you're screwing my wife in the same bed—but do you have to use my ass as a scoreboard?"

•

Hear about the bargain-hunter who got his vasectomy at Sears?

Every time he gets a hard-on, the garage door goes up.

•

Very horny but also very broke, Sam managed to scrape up two bucks and walk down to the local whorehouse. Looking at his meager offering, the madam burst out laughing. But being a good-natured sort, she informed him that there was in fact a special room for customers on a tight budget. Sam nodded gratefully, and was shown into a small, grimy room containing only a full-length mirror and a duck. "No way am I going to fuck a duck," he thought to himself. But after a while his horny state got the better of him, and, figuring he'd try anything once, he went for the duck.

A week later Sam was even hornier, but this time he had only a dollar to his name. "Sorry, buddy, but you can't get laid for a buck," the madam informed him, "but you can see a good show." Sam handed over his money and was led to a room in which several men were looking through a one-way window and roaring at the spectacle of a man getting it on with a nanny goat. Recalling last week's experience and feeling vaguely uncomfortable, Sam said defensively, "I don't see what's so funny, fellas."

One of the spectators turned to him. "You've got a point. Last week we had a guy doing it with a duck, and *that* was a riot!"

•

"Mr. Teller, I don't like the way your wife looks," the gynecologist began gravely.

"You should try the other end, doctor," interrupted Teller. "She's got a really cute face."

•

What's 68?

That's when she goes down on you and you owe her one.

•

DeFiore took up golf and was very proud of his new hobby. "Why, last week my boss and I played golf in the snow," he boasted to his girlfriend.

"Yeah? You have to paint your balls?" she asked.

"Nah," he replied offhandedly. "We wore long johns."

•

Did you hear about the man who had a terrible accident at the golf course?

He fell off the ball washer.

•

What's hard and straight going in, soft and sticky coming out?

Chewing gum.

•

What's six inches long that women love?

Folding money.

•

What are three words you never want to hear when you're making love?

"Honey, I'm home!"

•

Why do women like to play Pac-Man?

Because they can get eaten three times for a quarter.

•

Little Red Riding Hood was strolling through the woods on the way to visit her grandmother when suddenly the Big Bad Wolf jumped out from behind a tree. Licking his sharp white teeth, he snarled ferociously, "Now little girl, I'm going to eat you all up."

"Eat, eat, eat!" snapped Little Red Riding Hood disgustedly. "doesn't anyone fuck anymore?

•

Why is life like a penis?

Because when it's soft it's hard to beat, but when it's hard you get screwed.

•

From within the confessional the priest was having a very hard time eliciting the comely and bashful young girl's full confession. Finally he asked her to withdraw into his chambers. "Did the young man do this to you?" asked the priest kindly, putting one arm around the girl's shoulders.

"Yes, Father," admitted the young penitent.

"I see," murmured the priest, and bent to kiss her. "And did he do this?"

"Yes, Father, and worse," said the girl, blushing a bit.

"Did he do this?" The priest lifted her skirt, pulled down her panties, and began fingering her.

"Mmmmhmmm," confirmed the girl, now turning scarlet. "And worse."

"Something like this?" quizzed the priest. Thoroughly aroused and panting heavily, he pulled the girl down onto his divan, tore off his cassock, and proceeded to enter her vigorously. "Did he manage this, too?"

"Yes, Father, and worse," the girl told him when he had finished.

"This too, and worse?" asked the puzzled clergyman. "My dear child, what more terrible deed could the young man possibly have perpetrated?"

"You see, Father," explained the shy young penitent, "I think he's given me gonorrhea."

•

Definition of a diaphragm:
A trampoline for schmucks.

•

How do you know God meant men to eat pussy?
Why else would He have made it look like a taco?

•

Why do women fake orgasms?
Because they think men care.